Living With ADHD

A Comprehensive Guide for Men and Women with Adult ADHD to Achieve Emotional Control, Boost Productivity, Enhance Relationships, and Attain Success in Life.

Eric Holt

ISBN: 9781835123195

Contents

Introduction

F ocusing on work is difficult; you feel easily distracted and absentminded, you have trouble managing your time, and you can't focus for a sufficient amount of time. If any of the aforementioned rings a bell, you are not alone.

According to studies, 2.5 percent of adults and 8.4 percent of children are thought to have ADHD (Attention Deficit Hyperactivity Disorder). It is a prevalent condition that can affect both adults and children. Simple signs include fidgeting or squirming, excessive talking, difficulty relaxing or playing quietly, and difficulty sitting still. This can also be to blame for temper tantrums or outbursts of anger caused by failing to control strong emotions. It's crucial to remember that impulsivity, hyperactivity, and inattention symptoms do not necessarily indicate ADHD.

Making your payments on time, managing your family, career, and social obligations, and keeping up with everything else can be hard if you have ADHD, also called ADD. Adults with ADHD may experience difficulties in all facets of life, including relationships at home, work, and health. Extreme procrastination, difficulty meeting deadlines, and impulsive behavior could all be caused by your symptoms. Additionally, you can think your loved ones don't understand your challenges.

Fortunately, there are methods you can learn to control your ADHD symptoms. You can develop routines that improve your ability to operate more efficiently, keep organized, and interact with people. You can also learn to recognize your abilities and play to them. Helping yourself can involve explaining what you're going through to others.

However, change won't happen overnight. This self-help approach to ADHD needs tenacity, stamina, and, most importantly, a positive perspective. Utilizing these strategies increases your self-worth and makes you more productive, organized, and responsible. We created this guide to help you understand ADHD from start to finish because adults are currently the age group obtaining diagnoses at the quickest rate (to the point that some specialists are concerned it might be over-diagnosed). Let's begin.

1

Understanding Adult ADHD

A dults are now diagnosed with Attention Deficit Hyper-activity Disorder (ADHD) or Attention Deficit Disorder (ADD) more often and sometimes very late. What are the effects on people with the disorder, and what assistance can the doctor or pharmacist provide?

For people of a certain age, ADHD means hyperactive kids who may be American and taking Ritalin. It, therefore, comes as a shock when peculiar behaviors they had displayed their entire lives are identified as ADHD, a neurodiverse condition. Contrary to popular belief, there are more people in this category.

How many, then?

According to official statistics, the number of individuals receiving prescriptions for ADHD medication has sharply increased in the US over the past four years, increasing treatment for the condition by 80%. The prevalence of ADHD in US adults is also estimated by the Centers for Disease Control and Prevention (CDC) to be between 3 and 4%, with a 3 to 1 male-to-female ratio.

According to the same source, 3-6 out of every 100 school-aged children have ADHD, and 1 in 8 will continue to have it as adults. Given that approximately 338 million individuals live in the US, roughly 20 million of them, or more, have ADHD.

What Is Adult ADHD?

ADHD is a condition characterized by inattention, hyperactivity, and impulsivity. Adult ADHD is simply ADHD, as you might have assumed, but in adults.

While the symptoms are the same in adults and children, the manifestations can vary. Symptoms include forgetfulness, restlessness, trouble focusing, anger and emotional instability, rebellious behaviors, and loud, disruptive tendencies are more common in youngsters.

Adults may exhibit disorganization, poor time management, low-stress tolerance, agitation and anxiety, forgetfulness, loss of attention, a sense of being propelled by a motor, or the inability to sit still.

To put that into context, kids with ADHD might daydream a lot, act out during quiet time, interrupt people inappropriately, and have a room that looks like a disaster area.

It can be more difficult to spot in adults because the symptoms closely resemble burnout and stress, which practically everyone experiences these days.

Adults with ADHD may change jobs or relationships often, struggle to keep track of their schedules regularly (not just during busy times), be overly critical of themselves or have low self-esteem, and have trouble falling asleep or relaxing (i.e., the person who is multitasking while watching Netflix, reading a book, and checking email at the same time).

Adult men and women may also experience the symptoms of ADHD in various ways. Men often express hyperactive traits, while women with ADHD show calmer inattentive traits. They can forget to carry out their plans or feel perpetually overburdened by a long list of tasks they cannot complete.

The Prevalence Of ADHD In Men And Women

Are men or women more likely to have ADHD? This is a difficult answer. According to CDC, 12.9% of men and boys and 5.6% of girls and women have ADHD.

However, these data may understate the extent of the impact on women and girls.

Although it is underdiagnosed in girls for various reasons, ADHD is just as common among them.

Diagnosis

Even when their symptom profiles are identical, boys and men are more likely than girls and women to be referred for services, which results in greater diagnostic rates for boys and men.

According to a 2019 study, female patients may be more susceptible to having their ADHD diagnosis missed throughout the diagnostic procedure.

Women are less likely to be diagnosed with ADHD and be prescribed medication since they don't often exhibit the disruptive outward symptoms linked with the disorder.

We have seen that varying diagnosis rates are often linked to variables like cultural and gender prejudices and expectations due to our experience working with people who have ADHD and living with it.

According to research, women and girls are more prone to receive incorrect diagnoses for other mental health diseases, such as bipolar disorder, personality disorders, sadness, and anxiety, due to a lack of knowledge about ADHD in these groups.

The diagnosing process for adults might be difficult because it must be done thoroughly. People must consider comorbidities, trauma, medical issues, etc., as they seek a diagnosis later in life.

Usually, someone who needs ADHD testing will be referred by a mental or medical health expert. After that, they'll complete a psychiatric evaluation and several cognitive testing procedures to get a diagnosis.

The Starting Age

ADHD symptoms can appear as early as 2 to 3 years old; however, they usually appear before 12.

Because of how the symptoms express themselves, boys typically begin earlier than girls. According to a 2021 study on adult-onset ADHD, symptoms that appear later in life may be brought on by childhood problems that weren't treated by a doctor, among other things.

Although symptoms might change over time, especially with an early diagnosis and effective treatment, ADHD is a lifelong neurodevelopmental illness, meaning people don't "grow out of it."

Teenage years bring about hormonal changes that, if left untreated, can cause symptoms to worsen. For instance, variations in estrogen levels might influence the severity and manifestation of ADHD symptoms at several life phases, including puberty, the monthly menstrual cycle, perimenopause, and menopause.

We have observed that, particularly in recent years, the diagnostic rate among women (between the ages of 30 and 45) has been rising quickly due to pandemic-related changes in structure and environment.

Symptoms

Depending on a person's gender, age, and other traits, there are different ADHD symptoms. I don't think there are appreciable variations between men's and women's symptoms.

Due to structural and functional differences between the male and female brains, behaviors and presentations of the same ailments differ.

ADHD Signs In Females And Young Girls

Women are less likely to exhibit external hyperactivity and impulsivity than men. Women who experience internal hyperactivity often overthink, have intrusive thoughts, and engage in negative self-talk.

Other internalized signs of inattentiveness, distractibility, and hyperactivity in females and girls with ADHD may include maladaptive daydreaming, anxiety, depression, dozing off during conversations, easily losing focus, auditory processing disorder, forgetfulness, eating disorders, hypersexuality, impatience, body-focused repetitive behaviors (like skin picking, hair pulling, leg bouncing), exhaustion, insomnia, crying out with intense emotion, anger, and feelings of guilt.

Perfectionism, people-pleasing, codependency, body dysmorphia or a negative body image, low self-esteem, overachievement or underachievement, strong emotional reactivity, and overload are further signs of rejection-sensitive dysphoria (RSD).

ADHD Signs In Boys And Men

On the other hand, men and boys with ADHD are more likely to exhibit outward signs of the disorder, such as hyperactivity (e.g., fidgeting), disruptive behavior, always losing things, interrupting others during conversations, aggressive behaviors, and high-risk behaviors (e.g., substance abuse, speeding, unhealthy sexual behavior, excessive spending).

RSD can manifest in guys with the same severity as in women. Low self-esteem and insecurities can also affect men, although they typically manifest as the following: anger, indifference, self-centeredness, appearing uncaring of others' feelings, making fun of others or being sarcastic, trying to be right or disproving others' assertions, and defensiveness.

Males who experience elevated emotions or emotional dysregulation may exhibit more tantrums and outbursts of anger.

Many men are emotionally sensitive, and due to gender bias, they feel ashamed for this because it goes against society's expectations that men should "be tough or strong."

How ADHD May Be Affecting Your Life

The obstacles of living with attention-deficit hyperactivity disorder (ADHD) can make life more challenging and confusing. People with ADHD could even doubt whether they can lead a typical life. Fortunately, ADHD is easier to treat and maintain than other conditions once the issue is identified. ADHD might even boost your creativity, which could help you succeed in professions that call for new ideas or ways of thinking.

Being an adult with ADHD might make concentrating on work or conversations challenging. Some people could mistakenly assume that someone with ADHD is disorganized, sloppy, or lazy based on their behavior. People with ADHD may find it more difficult to form relationships and perform well at work due to this stigma.

Compulsive Eating

When you have ADHD, it's common to find it difficult to control your behavior, such as eating. Additionally, ADHD often causes dopamine levels, a hormone in your brain's pleasure area, to drop. You can temporarily increase your dopamine levels and regain that positive feeling by overeating.

Anxiety

Anxiety is indicated by persistent worry that prevents you from living the life you want. An anxiety condition coexists with ADHD in adults in about half of cases. Your symptoms of ADHD can occasionally make you feel tense. In that situation, managing your ADHD also lessens your anxiety.

Use Of Illicit Drugs

The same "thrill-seeking" tendencies that cause uncontrolled eating can also contribute to excessive and improper use of drugs and alcohol. Medical professionals say drug or alcohol use disorders and ADHD may be related.

Chronic Stress

Your ADHD symptoms can be stressful. When you have the disorder, your stress level is probably higher than the average over a longer period. Stress might eventually cause other problems like muscle strain and pain, breathing difficulties, heart problems, difficulty controlling blood sugar, and digestive problems.

Sleep Issues

ADHD may hamper your sleep. It increases your risk of snoring, sleep apnea, and restless legs syndrome, which causes you to feel the urge to move your legs when lying still. It may also throw off the circadian rhythm, your body's internal clock. That indicates that your sleep is out of phase with the sun's normal rising and setting. As a result, you may find it difficult to wake up and fall asleep at regular times.

Employment Issues

While every workplace is different, most of them demand that you show there on time, be attentive, focused, and organized, and do the assigned task. These can all be made more difficult by ADHD. As a result, you might not be able to meet your employer's expectations. So, keeping a job can be difficult.

Challenges With Deadlines

You may become forgetful and inattentive due to ADHD. Because of your focus issues, you probably also struggle with time management. Missed deadlines for tasks for work, school, and personal projects are possible effects of all of these symptoms.

Uncontrolled Spending

Purchasing goods just out of want temporarily elevates your "feel-good" chemicals. But there might be a cost for that. Your impulsive spending may leave you with a depleted bank account or damaged credit.

Financial Problems

Missing deadlines and engaging in risky spending habits are only two behaviors that increase your risk of not paying your debts on time. Maintaining your checkbook and paper statements are additional responsibilities that are more difficult when your ADHD symptoms are out of control.

Screen Dependence

ADHD indeed makes maintaining focus difficult. But the rapid changing of images, comments, graphics, and games on cellphones, video games, and televisions can capture your interest. It can be challenging to pull yourself away from a screen since your brain desires the reward it receives when you're there.

Sexual Issues

If you experience symptoms of ADHD while having sex, it can be very upsetting. You risk losing focus on your partner and the event as a whole. You might not be able to complete the journey if you lack patience. A successful sex life also requires effective communication, which may be difficult for you.

Relationship Difficulties

Couples who share an ADHD diagnosis often experience communication issues, especially if the symptoms are not being treated. When your partner tries to deal with certain aspects of your personality, such as forgetfulness or lack of attention, it could feel like they are always bugging you.

Emotional Lapses

One way that ADHD changes your brain is by making it more difficult for you to control your responses to situations. You can lose control and lash out in frustration or anger. It might also be the reason you obsess over such little matters.

2

Diagnosing Adult ADHD

Although there isn't a single medical, physical, or genetic test for ADHD, a skilled mental health care practitioner or doctor who compiles data from several sources can offer a diagnostic evaluation. These sources include standardized behavior rating scales, checklists of symptoms associated with ADHD, a thorough account of past and present functioning, and information gathered from loved ones or close companions who are familiar with the subject. To rule out a possible learning disability, some practitioners will assess cognitive ability and academic accomplishment. ADHD cannot be accurately diagnosed with a brief office visit or a simple talk with the patient. During the clinic appointment, the patient might not always show signs of ADHD; thus, the diagnostician must conduct a detailed life history. When making an ADHD diagnosis, co-occurring disorders must be taken into account.

The DSM-5 (Diagnostic and Statistical Manual of Mental Disorders, Fifth Edition), written by the American Psychiatric Association, contains clinical recommendations for diagnosing ADHD. These accepted guidelines are often applied in both clinical practice and research. The physician will try to ascertain whether these symptoms are still present in the adult and whether they were present in childhood during an evaluation. Adults must exhibit at least five of the symptoms to be diagnosed. The presentations of these symptoms in adults may differ from those in children because they can change with time.

The DSM-5 identifies three forms of ADHD: Hyperactive-Impulsive, Predominantly Inattentive, and Combined. Each condition's symptoms are modified and listed below.

ADHD Primarily Manifests As Inattentive Behavior

Has trouble maintaining focus, doesn't seem to listen, struggles to follow directions, avoids or dislikes tasks requiring sustained mental effort, struggles with organization, loses things, is easily distracted, and is forgetful in daily activities.

ADHD Is Primarily Manifested As An Impulsive Behavior

Acts as if driven by a vehicle. Adults will often feel inside as though a motor drives them; Talks excessively; Blurts out answers before questions have been fully answered; Have difficulty waiting or taking turns; Intrude or interrupting others; Has difficulty remaining seated; Extreme restlessness in adults; Runs around or climbs excessively in children; Difficulty engaging in activities quietly.

Combined Presentation Of ADHD

Both the inattention and hyperactive-impulsive ADHD presentations apply to the person. The presentations of these symptoms in adults may differ from those in children because they can change with time.

The physician diagnoses ADHD based on the severity and number of symptoms, the duration of symptoms, and how these symptoms hinder functioning at home, school, work, friends and family, or other activities. It is possible to have ADHD without exhibiting any signs of impulsivity or hyper-activity. The clinician must also ascertain whether co-existing conditions bring on or affect these symptoms.

A few of the symptoms had to be present before age 12. Typically, a parent or other informant is needed to confirm this. Significant impairment in at least two vital areas of the person's life is crucial to diagnosing ADHD; it is important to emphasize. The term "impaired" describes how ADHD affects a person's life. Examples of impairment include losing a job due to symptoms of ADHD, going through a lot of stress and distress in a marriage, running into financial difficulties as a result of impulsive spending, failing to make bill payments on time, or being placed on academic probation in college due to poor grades. A person might not meet the requirements for an ADHD clinical disorder diagnosis if they show signs of the illness but do not significantly impede them.

Web-Based Rating Scales

There are a lot of websites on the Internet about ADHD that include different kinds of surveys and lists of symptoms. Most of these tests are not standardized or scientifically proven; thus, they shouldn't be used to diagnose ADHD in oneself or others. Only a qualified, legally licensed practitioner may offer a reliable diagnosis.

Who Can Make The Diagnosis Of ADHD?

A doctor or a licensed mental health expert should perform an ADHD diagnostic evaluation for adults. Clinical psychologists, doctors (psychiatrists, neurologists, family doctors, or another sort of physician), or clinical social workers are some of these professionals.

Whichever professional type is selected, it's critical to enquire about their education and experience dealing with adults with ADHD. An accurate diagnosis and an effective treatment strategy are often more dependent on the professional's level of knowledge and skill about adult ADHD than the specific professional degree. Professionals with the necessary qualifications are typically open to sharing details about their education and work with people with ADHD. Reluctance to do so in response to legitimate inquiries can be seen with suspicion and may be a sign that the person should consult with another expert.

How Do I Find A Professional Experienced In ADHD Diagnosis?

Request a recommendation from your primary care physician for a local healthcare provider with the training and experience necessary to assess adults for ADHD. Calling a nearby university-affiliated hospital, a medical school, or a graduate psychology program for recommendations can also be beneficial. Visiting and speaking with group members might be beneficial if there is an ADHD support group in your region. Many probably have experience working with one or more professionals in your neighborhood and can share information with them. Most insurance plans include a list of specialists by specialization and can help customers who take part in their plans locate a healthcare provider. The professional directory of CHADD is one of the numerous websites that identify providers of ADHD services.

How Do I Know If I Need An ADD/ADHD Evaluation?

Most adults who want an assessment for ADHD have serious issues in one or more aspects of daily life. Some of the most common issues include inconsistent performance in careers or jobs; losing or quitting jobs often; a history of academic and career underachievement; a lack of ability to manage day-to-day responsibilities, such as finishing household tasks, maintenance tasks, paying bills, or organizing things; relationship issues as a result of not completing tasks; forgetting important details or becoming easily upset over minor things; and chronic stress and worry.

An expert can establish whether ADHD, another factor, or a mix of factors bring on these issues. Even though certain ADHD signs are visible as early as childhood, some people may not have serious issues until much later in life. For instance, some gifted people might mask their ADHD symptoms and don't have serious issues until they are in high school, college or are pursuing a job. In other situations, parents may have provided an extremely safe, orderly, and supportive environment, reducing the effects of ADHD symptoms until the child or young adult has started to live independently.

What Should I Do To Get Ready For The Evaluation?

Most people have some anxiety and trepidation before having any kind of condition, such as ADHD, tested. This is typical and shouldn't deter people from being tested if they think they might have ADHD or are experiencing serious problems. Unfortunately, many people are reluctant to seek help due to some of the widespread misconceptions about ADHD, such as the notions that "it only affects children" or "the person is just looking for an excuse."

Reviewing old report cards and other educational records from kindergarten or preschool can be valuable to many professionals. If such documents are accessible, they must be brought to the first consultation. You should also bring copies of any test results from earlier psychological evaluations to the appointment. Job assessments for individuals who have issues at work should be brought in for review if they are accessible.

Before the evaluation, many experts will ask the subject to complete and submit questionnaires and to name a spouse or other family member who can also participate in certain aspects of the evaluation. The evaluation will go more quickly if the questionnaires are completed and returned on time.

What Is A Comprehensive Evaluation?

Certain protocols are necessary for a thorough evaluation, even though different physicians will use slightly different testing methods and procedures. The DSM-5 symptom checklists, standardized behavior rating scales for ADHD, a thorough diagnostic interview, information from independent sources like the spouse or other family members, information from the spouse, and other types of psychometric testing as the physician deems required are among them. Below, we go into greater detail about these.

A Diagnostic Interview - Signs Of ADHD

An in-depth history of the person is given during a structured or semi-structured interview, which is the most crucial component of an exhaustive ADHD evaluation. The interviewer uses a predetermined, standardized set of questions to increase reliability and reduce the likelihood that a new interviewer might reach a different conclusion. The physician covers many topics, details pertinent issues, and asks follow-up questions to ensure all relevant topics are covered. The examiner will review the diagnostic standards for ADHD and assess how many of them, both currently and going back to childhood, apply to the subject. The extent to which these ADHD symptoms interfere with the person's life will also be determined during the interview.

Checking For Further Psychiatric Disorders During The Diagnostic Interview

The examiner will also perform a thorough evaluation to check for any other psychiatric conditions similar to ADHD or often co-occur with it. Research has indicated that more than two-thirds of people with ADHD have one or more co-existing conditions, and ADHD rarely happens alone. The most prevalent ones include substance use disorders, learning difficulties, anxiety disorders, and depression. Numerous of these disorders have symptoms resembling ADHD and can even be confused. Co-existing conditions are screened for as part of a thorough evaluation. Any co-occurring conditions must be identified and treated when they coexist with ADHD. Ineffective treatment of co-existing illnesses often results in ineffective treatment of ADHD. Importantly, failing to recognize this might lead to improper ADHD treatment for the patient when the symptoms of ADHD are a side effect of depression, anxiety, or another mental disease. In other instances, managing ADHD will take care of the secondary disorder and eliminate the need to manage it separately from ADHD.

The examiner may also inquire about the subject's medical history, early development, academic and professional experiences, driving record, history of drug and alcohol misuse, family and marital status, and social history. The examiner will search for patterns that are typical of people with ADHD while also attempting to identify potential causes of symptoms that resemble ADHD.

Participation Of Family Members

The doctor must speak with one or more independent sources, typically a close relative (spouse, parent, partner, or family member) familiar with the patient. This process does not intend to cast doubt on the subject's sincerity but rather elicit more details. Many adults with ADHD have hazy or subpar memories, especially from childhood. They could remember certain details, but they might not remember the diagnoses or issues they faced. As a result, the physician might ask the person undergoing evaluation to have their parents complete a retrospective ADHD profile outlining behavior from childhood.

Many adults with ADHD could be only dimly aware of how their behaviors affect others and themselves. Couples who are married or living together will benefit from the clinician interviewing them jointly when reviewing the ADHD symptoms. This approach sets the basis for relationship improvement when the diagnostic process is complete by helping the non-ADHD partner or spouse develop an accurate understanding and sympathetic attitude toward the impact of ADHD symptoms on the relationship. If it is impossible to interview the family members, having them complete symptom checklists is a good substitute.

Many adults with ADHD may experience extreme frustration and shame due to the constant issues brought on by the condition. It is crucial that the person undergoing evaluation openly and honestly share these issues and does not withhold information out of embarrassment or concern for backlash. The correctness of the information presented to the examiner will play a significant role in the evaluation's quality and the precision of the diagnosis and treatment suggestions.

Standardized Methods Of Rating Behavior

A thorough evaluation may use one or more standardized behavior rating measures. Research comparing the behaviors of those with ADHD and those without ADHD is used in these questions. Rating scale results, though not considered diagnostic in and of themselves, are a crucial source of factual data used in the evaluation process. Most therapists ask the subject of the evaluation and the subject's close relationship to complete these rating measures.

More Testing

Additional psychiatric, neuropsychological, or learning difficulties testing may be required, depending on the person and the issues being addressed. Although they cannot accurately diagnose ADHD, they can offer valuable insight into how it affects the individual. Co-existing conditions' presence and consequences can also be ascertained through tests. For instance, the clinician will typically administer an intellectual ability test and an academic success test to ascertain whether the person has a learning problem.

Inspection Of The Body

A medical examination is advised to rule out medical explanations for symptoms if the person being assessed has not had a recent physical examination (within the last 6 to 12 months). The symptoms of other medical disorders, such as thyroid issues and seizure disorders, might resemble those of ADHD. While a medical exam cannot prove ADHD, it is crucial in helping the exclusion of other disorders or issues.

Finalizing The Assessment

A written summary or report will be completed after the evaluation, and the clinician will give the person and family their diagnostic opinions regarding ADHD and any other psychiatric disorders or learning disabilities that may have been discovered during the evaluation. After reviewing treatment options, the clinician will work with the patient to develop an effective medical and psychosocial intervention strategy. The clinician will then consult the patient's primary care doctors as necessary.

Strategies For Finding The Right Healthcare Professional

ADHD can make it challenging for people to focus and regulate their behavior. One of the most prevalent chronic disorders in children, it affects between 3% and 5% of the population.

Where do you begin if you or your child has ADHD and need a specialist's help? There are numerous varieties of specialists, each with a specific field of expertise. Here are some pointers on how to locate the ideal candidate for you.

Choosing An ADHD Specialist To Contact

First, get a recommendation from your primary care physician. They will probably have a list of experts knowledgeable about ADHD and can help treat it.

There are various possibilities for finding a specialist if you don't have a regular physician or wish to consider other options. To start, search online. Numerous doctor directories include details on specialties and areas of focus. Another choice is to seek recommendations from friends or relatives. They might be familiar with an expert who has assisted them or know someone who has.

Finally, give your neighborhood mental health facility or ADHD support group a call. They often include a list of local experts that can assist.

No matter how you locate a professional, speaking with several before choosing one is crucial. Inquire about their expertise in treating ADHD, their techniques, and the outcomes they've experienced. It's crucial that you feel at ease with the expert and that they know your needs. You can obtain the help you require to manage your ADHD from the appropriate professional.

Effectiveness Of ADHD Treatment

Treatment for ADHD can be useful in easing symptoms and enhancing performance. The most extensively researched treatment for ADHD is stimulant medication, which has been demonstrated to be beneficial in easing symptoms in 70% to 80% of users.

Treatments such as behavior therapy, in addition to medication, can be effective in treating the signs of ADHD. People with ADHD are given techniques in behavior therapy to help them manage their symptoms. It may work well for taming impulses, streamlining tasks, and boosting self-control.

The average length of time for treating ADHD is several months to years. Working with a specialist is crucial because they can monitor your symptoms and help you identify the best course of action for you or your child. People with ADHD can live fulfilling lives if given the right care.

Different Types Of ADHD Experts

Several types of specialists can help treat ADHD. Here are a few examples:

- **Neuropsychologists** - Neuropsychologists are experts in identifying and treating brain-related issues. They can help those who have ADHD in recognizing and controlling their symptoms.

- **Clinical Psychologists** - Clinical psychologists are experts in treating mental health conditions via therapy. They can help those who have ADHD in controlling their symptoms and learning coping mechanisms.

- **ADHD Coaches** - These professionals are skilled in helping those with the disorder manage their symptoms and achieve their goals. They can help you stay on track with your goals by offering advice, encouragement, and support.

- **Pediatricians -** Pediatricians treat ADHD in children and are experts in young people's health. They can also suggest medical professionals who can help in treating adult ADHD.

- **Specialist Physicians -** A variety of specialists are available to help treat ADHD. Pediatric developmental doctors, neurologists, and psychiatrists are a few examples. Before choosing, it's crucial to speak with multiple experts.

Who Should Make The Diagnoses For ADHD?

The best person to diagnose ADHD is typically a psychiatrist or other mental health expert who specializes in the disorder. However, the diagnosis might also be made by your family physician.

It's crucial to receive an accurate diagnosis to receive the best care. Talk to your mental health expert or doctor if you believe you or your kid may have ADHD. They can assist you in determining the situation and whether ADHD is the appropriate diagnosis.

If I Have ADHD, Should I See A Psychiatrist Or Psychologist?

The optimal treatment for ADHD will differ from person to person, so there is no universally applicable answer to this question. There is a misperception that only psychologists provide treatment, and psychiatrists simply administer medicine. This, however, is untrue.

A psychiatrist can recommend counseling and medication to people with ADHD. Or, a person might visit a psychiatrist (for treatment and medicine) and a psychologist (only for therapy). Social workers are one example of mental health professionals who can offer treatment.

Speak to your usual doctor or a mental health professional if you are unsure who to visit. They can help you select the best professional for your needs.

How Do I Pick An ADHD Psychologist?

It's crucial to locate a psychologist knowledgeable about ADHD and with expertise in treating it while searching for someone to help you with your condition. You can check online or in doctor directories or ask your usual physician for a recommendation.

You must feel at ease working with the psychologist you select. You should have confidence in them and feel they understand your circumstance and who you are. Try looking for a different psychologist if you don't think this one is a suitable fit. You should be able to discover an effective specialist because several focus on treating ADHD.

How To Locate A Coach For ADHD

You might want to think about working with an ADHD coach if you need help controlling your ADHD. Coaches have special training to help ADHD patients manage their symptoms and achieve their goals.

Finding a coach that is a good fit for you is crucial because there are numerous different types of coaches. A coach can be located online or through professional directories. It's also crucial to speak with numerous coaches before choosing one.

To better manage their ADHD, some people may find it helpful to work with coaches. They can help you stay on track with your goals by offering advice, encouragement, and support.

How To Help Someone In Locating An ADHD Expert

You may do a few things to help someone else find the best doctor if you're looking for a specialist for them.

Discuss the person's requirements for a specialist and their demands with them. Assist them in researching various medical professionals and enquiring about their experience with ADHD; if you can, go with them to consultations with suitable specialists.

Encourage them to keep looking until they find a doctor who best fits them.

Finding the appropriate ADHD specialist can be challenging, but obtaining the right care is important. You can successfully control your ADHD symptoms with the right support.

3
Strategies For Emotional Control

Anyone who has heard of attention-deficit hyperactivity disorder (ADHD) knows that individuals with this condition have difficulty focusing and managing their attention. What is less generally known is that ADHD can also make it difficult to regulate one's emotions, a condition called emotional dysregulation in psychology.

According to clinical studies, emotional dysregulation affects as many as 70% of individuals with ADHD. Nearly half of individuals with ADHD receive treatment for depression at some point, and more than 50% have an anxiety disorder. ADHD is also often accompanied by abrupt, uncontrolled angry outbursts.

Let's start by answering the more basic question before discussing how to deal with emotional dysregulation: What exactly does "emotional regulation" mean? A person can prevent overreacting to emotionally charged situations by exercising emotional management. It enables individuals to control their emotional outbursts and react to difficult events more consciously and calmly. A person's capacity for emotional regulation allows them to change their emotional state to make it more conducive to achieving their goals.

On the other hand, emotional dysregulation is the failure to match one's emotions with one's goals. Consider John, an office worker, as someone fighting for a promotion. His supervisor may hesitate to offer him additional responsibility if he often loses his cool in meetings. John will be more successful if he instead employs emotional regulation techniques to control his anger and deal with the symptoms of ADHD.

It should come as no surprise that emotional dysregulation in adults with ADHD is linked to a wide range of functional deficits. According to research, those who have trouble controlling their emotions are more likely to hurt themselves or others. Additionally, they are more likely to fail out of school, get divorced, commit crimes, cause accidents, and make poor financial decisions.

What Causes Emotional Dysregulation In Adult ADHD?

Simply put, the pre-frontal cortex serves a crucial function in controlling emotions. Unfortunately, the prefrontal cortex does not work as well in adults with ADHD as in neurotypical individuals. It's a common metaphor to say that people with ADHD have a Ferrari brain and bicycle brakes. In other words, the ADHD brain finds it easy to accelerate but difficult to decelerate.

ADHD symptoms and some mood disorder symptoms are similar. For instance, commencing tasks is difficult for those with ADHD and clinical depression. According to some researchers, variations in specific brain areas (such as the amygdala and prefrontal cortex) may contribute to emotional dysregulation and other ADHD symptoms.

The effects of untreated ADHD symptoms can also result in or worsen emotional problems. An adult with ADHD who has not developed executive functioning skills, for instance, may occasionally forget deadlines. Stress arises naturally from the potential outcomes, which range from failing a college course to getting a poor performance review at work. They can increase the anxiety level of someone with ADHD beyond what they can manage. A person's sense of self-worth can be damaged by repeatedly going through unpleasant outcomes, which can also set them up for frustration and depression.

How To Regulate Emotions With ADHD

According to preliminary studies, therapy patients who specifically focus on their emotional dysregulation problems tend to have better outcomes. Ten emotional control techniques for adults with ADHD are provided below. We advise consulting with an ADHD specialist as you try these techniques and determine which ones are most effective for you.

Learn To Monitor Yourself

Keep an eye on yourself in both neutral and emotional circumstances. How quickly can you react? How would you describe your feelings? Does your reaction help you in achieving your objectives? Do you generally have a neutral disposition, or is there occasionally irritability?

Self-monitoring is the first step to properly managing emotional dysregulation because many people with this condition have trouble identifying their feelings.

Maintain Your Physical Well-Being

The consequences of sleep deprivation on adults are generally underestimated, despite everyone understanding that a tired toddler is a cranky toddler. Adults often hide their feelings. However, when we are sleepy, hungry, hot, cold, ill, etc., we get just as cranky on the inside as toddlers.

Get enough rest, work out often, and watch what you eat. You can support your psychological health and improve your capacity to handle stress by maintaining good physical health.

Learn Coping Mechanisms And ADHD Skills

According to research, a person's capacity to control their emotions improves as their ADHD symptoms do. If you consider it, this makes sense. There will be less cause for anger when your ADHD symptoms stop interfering with your life.

Make every effort to lessen the emotional toll that ADHD takes on your life.

Hold Onto Reality

We often have negative thoughts while we're under stress. We obsess over negative things that happened in the past and worry about the future. By centering yourself in the here and now, you can keep yourself from getting carried away by these negative thoughts.

The next time you notice yourself dwelling on the past or the future, direct your attention to your five senses and the environment around you. Use a guided meditation or a grounding technique. You might want to begin a daily mindfulness practice to stop uncontrollable negative thoughts and emotions from building up in the future.

Challenge Negative Thoughts

Negative thoughts might make me unhappy and anxious even when they don't match reality. It is crucial to challenge negative thoughts as soon as they surface.

For instance, if your friend doesn't reply to your text immediately, don't think they are upset with you. Consider whether they are busy or their phone's battery needs replacing. Believing someone when they say something regarding emotional control is usually a good idea.

The Use Of Medication

Although there is still much to learn, early research indicates that medication may help with emotional dysregulation. Treatment of ADHD symptoms with stimulant medication can improve emotional wellbeing since untreated ADHD symptoms can increase the stress a person must manage. Additionally, some psychiatrists advise using SSRIs or other mood-regulating medications to treat emotional problems immediately. To find drugs that treat your specific cluster of symptoms, speak with a professional psychiatrist and ADHD specialist.

Schedule Some Inspiring Activities

Often, a person's ability to control their mood is exceeded by a combination of stressors rather than just one. There is a limit to how much stress a person can handle before losing their cool.

Set yourself up for success by including activities to help you feel refreshed rather than letting stress and disappointments accumulate. Plan a relaxing activity or a half-hour each night if you have ADHD and anxiety. If depression has made you feel down, take a brief morning stroll, tune into a motivational podcast, or engage in any other energizing activity.

Consider Your Options Before Acting (Or "Do The Opposite" Of Your First Impulse)

While acting on your emotions while you're emotionally charged can lead to complications, all feelings are natural and valid. Ideally, before responding to whatever is troubling you, take a moment to gather your thoughts, relax, and consider your objectives. Nevertheless, if you have ADHD, it might seem impossible to wait before reacting.

I urge you to keep in mind our "do the opposite" method if you must act right away. Take any action completely at odds with your initial emotional instinct. For instance, give the woman who cut you off in traffic the peace sign instead of swearing at her! Even though it may seem foolish, this tactic has worked well for many people.

Develop Expertise In Something

This method works wonders for ADHD patients who experience depression or a sense of helplessness. Doing things, you enjoy helps you feel more confident and deserving of yourself. Doing what you love can lift your spirits and strengthen your fortitude. It will be easier for you to handle setbacks the more "mastery moments" you have.

Distance Yourself Emotionally From Challenging Situations

A new viewpoint can help emotional events lose some of their emotional impacts. Try putting more space between you and emotional stimuli to use this method. For instance, if the argument at the table next to you is making it difficult for you to study, move to a table further away.

Distancing can also be done in the future, for example, by picturing how you will laugh about an embarrassing incident when you tell your story. You could also put yourself at an objective distance. You might, for instance, consider how one of your finest and most sensible friends would respond if they were present and saw you being mistreated.

Why You Must Be Self-Aware Of Your ADHD To Take Action, Change, And Progress

By striving to accept who you are, how you think, and what makes your ADHD brain tick, you can unlock great power and productivity. Discover how to make the most of your strengths and develop the plans you require to complete tasks.

We want things to change, and we want them to change without any persistent effort on our part. Or we fight our ADHD brains, denying and resisting lifelong realities about how we perform well and how we do not. Or we overthink things to the point that we believe we truly did it. Knowing what to do doesn't make it happen. The core of the ADHD difficulty is the transition from knowing to action.

What then triggers genuine change and advancement? Recognizing (rather than fighting) the differences caused by

ADHD and accepting who we are. Maximizing our skills and creating workarounds when necessary is made easier by increasing our self-awareness and self-acceptance (the power of potential and choice!).

Understanding and utilizing our thought processes is essential for strategizing and acting productively. The more we understand the process of change, the easier it becomes. Here are some ways to begin the procedure.

Honesty Is The First Step To ADHD Self-Awareness

Making a list of your strengths and weaknesses, including who you are and are not, what you are likely to do or not, and how you operate versus how you wish you worked, is the first step in developing self-awareness. You run the risk of creating a life or acting in ways that won't work for you if you lack self-awareness. Knowing who you are and how you operate (or don't) will help you create tactics to maximize your abilities and compensate for your ADHD issues. You can take action to lessen your frustration triggers if you know them. When you know what gives you energy, you can arrange a time for it.

Angie became frustrated because she struggled to integrate exercise into her workday. She decided to go to the gym first thing every day. Although it was a terrific idea, it couldn't be maintained by someone who often had trouble getting out of bed and made it to work late. She enrolled in an after-work workout class but often skipped it due to her exhaustion from her job. We talked about more sensible options. She left the office for a yoga lesson in the middle of the day, which helped her focus and feel more energized later. She attended yoga with coworkers because it was a social activity, which made it easier to keep the commitment.

Practice ADHD Self-Acceptance

Even if you don't like aspects of yourself, accepting who you are and your thoughts and behaviors will increase your productivity.

Set up a space where there are no judgments, and let go of your expectations of yourself. You are a singular blend of your personality, background, ADD, LD, IQ, genetics, birth order, abilities, and surroundings. We are less inclined to react and can better act when we embrace ourselves. Break free from the self-critical guilt trap. Instead of allowing us to advance, guilt keeps us mired in a web of failure and regret. According to studies, those who accept themselves are happier and more successful.

Recognize Your Ability To Make Decisions

Accepting our difficulties does not preclude us from making changes. Stop thinking like a victim! Biology, history, environment, experiences, or other people may worsen our difficulties, but we always have a choice in how we react. Think about what we can do rather than what we can't. You might need to find a solution to a challenge, but the ADHD brain is great at it.

Have Faith In Your Ability To Think Differently

Do your beliefs have any restrictions? When evaluating a circumstance or your skills, are you realistic? Check your perspective. Never rely on your first impulse. Drama appeals to the brain. For us, everything must be either perfect or useless, all or nothing.

James was having trouble in college. He adopted the techniques we outlined and changed a number of his habits, but his academic performance remained unchanged. When I asked him if he thought he could succeed, he responded negatively. James felt he couldn't change, which put him in a bind. His grades and self-confidence increased as he tried to change his thinking.

Create A Road Map For Your Brain

Make your goals specific and believe in your ability to change your life. It is less likely that you will complete any of your goals if you try to complete too many at once. Even if you take pleasure in your capacity for multitasking, you cannot simultaneously catch two rabbits.

Aaron, a new coaching client of mine, had modified his sleep and waking cycles and was pleased to adhere to a plan to enhance his productivity, but he was irritated by his attempts to "master time." He burned out after a while of it working. Why? He tried to adopt behaviors that weren't compatible with his ADHD brain. Together, we looked into more practical options to help him adjust what he wanted (such as creating "white space" in his daily calendar for unexpected or downtime activities). His sleep/wake cycle gradually changed, and he adjusted. He had enough time for these new actions to become part of him. Less was more!

Plan Your Approach To Success!

Change happens when objectives are explicit, goals are attainable, and solutions are clear and realistic. Start by saying,

"I will leave the house by 8:15 every morning so that I can arrive at work relaxed and on time," instead of Aaron's, "I am going to master time."

The more you understand yourself, the easier it will be to create brain-friendly ADHD coping mechanisms. Consider that each assignment requires two different sets of tactics. The first step is to gather the resources, advice, and methods needed to complete the assignment; the second is to inspire yourself to finish it.

Act!

Consider what might prevent you from acting, whether external circumstances or internal worries (negative self-talk, avoidance, doubt, a lack of enthusiasm or conviction). Have backup plans in place, and always be gentle to yourself. You'll be more equipped to complete tasks if you know and understand how your ADHD brain works.

Free Goodwill

D ear fellow traveler on the ADHD journey,

Before we move on to the next chapter, I want to congratulate you on your bravery in seeking help and support to deal with the particular difficulties that come with ADHD. You have made a huge step toward realizing your potential and leading a satisfying life by accepting your journey and actively seeking knowledge.

I invite you to share your experiences and knowledge with others with ADHD. Those who want to gain emotional control, increase productivity, create meaningful connections, and flourish personally and professionally can use your experiences and insights as a lighthouse.

By leaving an honest review of this book, you become a source of inspiration for other ADHD pathfinders. Your comments have the power to inspire and motivate others, demonstrating to them that despite having ADHD, they can still thrive and achieve success.

Share the techniques that have connected with you the most, the epiphanies you have had, and the amazing progress you have made in gaining emotional control, increasing productivity, improving relationships, and achieving success. Your review can inspire people to embrace their skills, overcome obstacles, and live their best lives with ADHD by giving them hope and advice.

Let's work together to create an accepting community of people with ADHD committed to flourishing and realizing their dreams.

This is as easy as writing a review—a gesture that takes only a few seconds but has a big impact.

I appreciate you sharing your experience, wisdom, and suggestions. I wish you boundless strength, resilience, and remarkable achievement as you navigate living with ADHD and maximizing your potential.

With gratitude,

Eric Holt

4
Boosting Productivity With ADHD

W e've created a list of ADHD tips and methods to increase productivity, improve mood, get more sleep, and combat procrastination. Let's begin immediately.

Improving Productivity

- **A Wall Calendar -** A dry-erase wall calendar is useful for organizing your schedule. Time blindness is greatly alleviated by writing appointments and deadlines in bold colors and crossing off each day that passes.

- **Use Color -** People with ADHD are often visual learners. Highlight significant dates, color-code documents, write to-dos on colorful paper, and add stickers or color to practically everything that requires your attention to make things stick in your mind. You may also utilize color coding in Google Calendar to make items stand out.

- **Organize Tasks** - Do you have a target or due date? Along the process, establish smaller deadlines. This can make you feel more confident and less stressed.

- **Try The Pomodoro Technique** - Start working on your project, set the timer for 20 minutes, and then stop. Take a 5-minute rest after 20 minutes, then repeat. Put a checkmark next to each cycle you complete.

- **Reframing** - Reframe tasks constructively or more practically to combat negative mental habits. For instance, if you are putting off starting a project and your initial thinking is, "There is too much work; it'll take much time," try checking yourself with a less depressing and more realistic thought like, "If I start this today, I'll feel great, and there will be less work tomorrow."

- **24-Hour Hot Spot** - Set aside a space, such as your workstation, where you can keep track of your "need to-dos." Anything that requires your attention within the next 24 hours should be placed there to prevent loss.

- **Pocket Notes** - Writing vital things on notes and placing them in your pocket is a safer alternative to writing on your hands. Ensure it's in your dominant side pocket so you're more likely to reach in and retrieve your reminder.

- **Smartphone** - Get a smartphone) and use the calendar, notepad, and reminder alerts to help you fulfill deadlines. Set multiple obnoxious reminders in the days running up to your deadline.

Sleeping Better With ADHD

Set a wind-down alarm on your smartphone. Most smart-phones let you program a bedtime alarm that will alert you an hour before you plan to go to sleep. Use this signal to start your night ritual, turn off all electronics, and dim the lights.

- **Happy Lamp -** It might be challenging for many people with ADHD to sleep because of physiological variations in their circadian rhythms consistently. Your circadian rhythm can be improved by using a happy lamp or obtaining 20 minutes of early morning light exposure.

- **Melatonin -** Melatonin levels are often decreased in ADHD patients. Try a supplement (0.3mg is the recommended dosage) or eat foods that cause melatonin production, such as tart cherry juice.

- **No Late Lattes -** Caffeine takes up to 12 hours for your body to completely digest. Avoid caffeine 5-7 hours before bed to get a better night's sleep.

- **Calm Your Mind -** Is your mind racing and keeping you up? Progressive muscle relaxation is one approach that can help you relax and fall asleep.

- **Get Noisy -** Noise machines might increase sleep quality and duration, particularly pink noise (imagine rainfall and ocean waves).

- **Keep It Cool -** Lower the temperature in your room to 65–68°F (18–20°C), which is the optimum range for melatonin generation and sleep.

- **Regular Wake-Up Times -** The sleep-regulating system in your body benefits from regular waking-up times. Setting a regular wake time is the most practical strategy to keep a consistent schedule and control your sleep hormones.

- **Sleep Mask -** Use a sleep mask or blackout curtains to improve your sleep quality because melatonin production is maintained by darkness.

- **Only Utilize The Bed For Sleeping -** otherwise, connections such as bed + job, bed + scary movies, or bed + existential dread may be formed. Sleep therapists refer to this as stimuli control; only use your bed for sleep (and intimacy).

Getting Chores Done

- **Begin Small -** Allow yourself the luxury of minor tasks that bring your major goals closer to completion. Does the kitchen need cleaning? Start with a single countertop section. Progress is better than no progress. Always begin with one room at a time, and if necessary, focus on just one area of that room.

- **Apps -** Apps for managing your grocery lists include Out of Milk, which uses a basic scanning mechanism. Even family members can sync their lists with yours.

- **Calendar For Your Daily Routine At Home -** Make things easy by creating a list of tasks you can complete each week. To help you remember which tasks you need to complete on certain days, use a wall calendar and lots of colorful markers.

- **Let Your Plants Live** - Track your watering schedule using applications like Happy Plant to keep indoor plants alive.

- **20-Minute Rule** - The 20-minute rule states that you must wait 20 minutes before enjoying some "down-time" (such as a Netflix binge). Simply set a timer for 20 minutes and complete the assignment during that period. You can perform the same action repeatedly, such as organizing your room's clothing. If you have a spouse or children, see if you can turn it into a game.

- **Make It Enjoyable** - Although they may seem over-whelming, chores aren't all that unpleasant. Set the mood by playing upbeat music, donning an attractive "cleaning outfit," and concentrating on one activity at a time.

- **Invite Visitors Over** - Nothing inspires you to clean up like a visitor. Try to host dinner or drinks at least once a week, and use that as an incentive to tidy up.

- **Ask For Help** - If you're feeling overwhelmed, ask for assistance. Reaching out to a loved one might be less intimidating, and occasionally, you need a little motivation to start. Additionally, they might have the time to assist.

- **Put Fitness First** - Put on your pedometer and com-mit to using your daily duties as exercise.

- **Look For Expired Food** - Choose a day of the week to remove expired food from the refrigerator (you're starting to feel exposed, aren't you?).

Managing & Minimizing ADHD Impulsivity

- **The 24-Hour Rule** - The 24-hour rule states that you must always allow yourself a cooling-off period before making an impulsive choice or signing up for something. Try to wait at least 24 hours before getting started. If you genuinely "need" it, the desire remains.

- **What Will Become Of This?** - If you're compelled to buy anything while shopping, ask yourself, "Where will this live?" Stopping to consider where it fits into your life can result in a humble epiphany.

- **Before You Speak, Say It Again** - Impulsive actions are challenging to manage. Before responding, try to paraphrase what was stated while you were listening. It will not only clear up any possible misunderstandings but also allow you a moment to consider your reply.

- **Evaluate Yourself** - By outlining the circumstance, your feelings just before acting, and what you should do the next time to stop the impulsive behavior, you can practice naming your impulsivity. Consider it a problem that a logical scientist is attempting to solve.

- **Elastic Band** - Wrap your wrist in a rubber band and snap it whenever you impulse to act rashly. It's a method that can help end unwanted patterns and bring your senses back to the present.

- **Note It** - Take a moment to write it down before contributing to meetings or debates. Use a notepad or phone to quickly write down what you want to say and bring it up later if it's still important.

- **Meditate** - Practice daily meditation to strengthen your capacity to think things through before acting. You can begin with two to three minutes daily and work up to ten to twenty.

- **Exercise** - Daily activity is a great method to eliminate angst and restlessness, fueling impulsive actions. Aim to spend 20 minutes each day doing something you like. Even a daily walk is sufficient for significant advantages.

- **Practice Pausing** - When someone is speaking, try to listen intently to every word and then wait three seconds before responding. After practicing with a trusted companion, you can test it out in the wild.

- **Apologize** - Interruptions do occur. If you interrupt someone, recognize it, say you're sorry, and give them a chance to finish. Describe your motivation if you like.

Overcoming Procrastination

- **Lock Box** - One of the largest distractions, particularly for those with ADHD, is using a phone. Put your phone away with a timed lock box when you have important tasks! When you're done, Tik Tok will still be accessible.

- **Take A Look Around You** - Keeping a distraction-free environment clear is crucial for productivity. Keep the area clutter-free or cover distractions with baskets while you work.

- **Simply Do The Task At Hand** - Act as soon as you

can. The ADHD mind has difficulty refocusing when life becomes hectic, or there are distractions. Take a big breath, put on your disciplined pants, and just do the thing, no matter how annoying it might seem.

- **Get Stimulated** - ADHD minds often experience a lack of stimulation, which might cause them to forego monotonous jobs in favor of more fun ones. Include a slime kit, relaxing music, a fidget spinner, a workout, a podcast, or anything else that will get you moving. As long as pairing actions advance you closer to your goal, it's acceptable.

- **Try Combining L-Theanine With Caffeine** - Combining L-theanine with caffeine can increase caffeine's benefits on "focus" while calming anxiety. According to studies, this combination enhances the cognitive function and sustained attention of ADHD patients.

- **Positive Self-Talk** - Counter your negative inner voice with one that is upbeat. The maxims "I tried my best, and that's enough," "nothing is perfect, it's ok to be human," and "I am strong, capable, and I can get through anything" are good ones to try.

- **Hug Your Inner Child** - It's common for people with ADHD to feel misunderstood as children. A positive affirmation of your inner child from your adult self will greatly help. Give a gentle embrace of encouragement to your inner child. Try encouraging them and promising to do your best to support and understand them as they navigate life.

- **Clarify Your Objectives** - Define your ultimate goal,

then list the "mini" goals you must accomplish to reach it. Set a timeframe, concentrate on the first mini-goal, and focus solely on that. If you're still feeling overburdened, further divide your mini-goals. The idea is to start going forward simply.

Better Control Your Emotions

- **Schedule Downtime** - Allocate a period each week (or perhaps a certain time each day) to accomplish nothing. You can do whatever brings you delight: blast music, use your phone to drift off, or indulge in a pastime. Scheduling in this "do whatever I want" time gives much-needed downtime structure, preventing you from idly idling away hours and then feeling terrible.

- **Accept The Highs And Lows** - Accepting your feelings without passing judgment on them can be quite relieving. Whenever you experience great sadness, annoyance, or anxiety, try not to fight it or seek an explanation. Remind yourself that everything passes in time as you sit with the emotion and let the thoughts come and go without judging them. The worst that emotions can do is make you feel uncomfortable for a little while.

- **Keep A Journal** - Writing out your feelings and thoughts might help you process them and find peace daily or when angry.

- **Breathwork** - Anxiety, overwhelm, and frayed feelings are common concerns with ADHD. Try to concentrate on your breathing when you experience

these feelings and take a few slow, deep breaths
through your nostrils and mouth. Your parasympa-
thetic nervous system is stimulated, which reduces
the stress reaction in your body.

- **Take A Break** - When you feel irate, annoyed, over-
stimulated, or prepared to lash out, take a break. Take
a walk, sit quietly, put on some relaxing music in
your headphones, or do anything that makes you feel
peaceful. Feel free to withdraw from circumstances
so you can look after your mental health.

- **Learn To Be Polite** - How your brain is structured
makes it difficult to plan, pay attention, hold your
tongue, and carry out daily duties. When things go
wrong, try to open a discussion with yourself rather
than being rude to yourself. Consider using expressions like "OK, ADHD; you win this round."

- **Find Your Tribe** - Surrounding yourself with
like-minded individuals is crucial. Try sharing mate-
rials about ADHD with your present circle if they are
open to it, or describe what it's like for you. Online
forums, Instagram profiles, and support groups for
ADHD are resources you can use to feel heard and
understood.

- **Hire A Therapist** - Therapy can help develop
self-acceptance and emotional management skills.
Think of therapy as individualized brain training;
sometimes, you need a little direction to get things
in shape. Now that many internet possibilities exist,
treatment is more accessible and affordable than ever.

Self-Care

- **Determine Your Triggers** - It's critical to understand your triggers. Plan for the sounds, situations, and even individuals that make you feel stressed and frustrated. Simple solutions include having earplugs or head-phones at hand.

- **Plan A Meal** - Skipping meals and bingeing are bad habits that are difficult to change. No matter what, try your best to eat a protein-rich meal or drink in the morning. It will help control your hunger and ensure your body gets the ingredients necessary to produce substances like dopamine.

- **Hygiene** - Maintaining hygiene practices can be challenging, but at other times you're rocking 25-step skincare regimens. When you're struggling, try sim-plification, use dry shampoo, find an accountability partner, and be polite to yourself about the highs and lows.

- **Stains Happen** - ADHD causes stains; it's a life of stains. Save your favorite garments by learning how to remove stains effectively.

- **Include Yoga** - Even 10-15 minutes a day can signif-icantly impact your wellbeing and ability to handle frustration and stress.

- **Add This Affirmation** - You'll experience challeng-ing days occasionally. Try saying to yourself again, "Now is not forever. Be here now.

- **Practice Gratitude** - Create a reminder on your

phone to practice gratitude simultaneously daily. Stop what you're doing when it goes off, and consider something you are sincerely grateful for. Try to focus on it for only 60 seconds.

- **When You're Feeling Low, Indulge** - Permit yourself to wear a face mask, eat a hearty snack, and watch your favorite show. You should occasionally reward yourself for a romantic evening with yourself. Don't feel guilty about taking the time you require; you are not being selfish.

- **Create Boundaries** - It's challenging to refuse. Permit yourself to decline an invitation or withdraw if you agree to anything without giving it much thought to avoid exhausting yourself.

- **Remove Your Cape** - Being a superhero is entertaining, but you risk losing yourself. You are not required to take care of everyone or to be flawless. Try to be realistic about how much balancing you can manage, and keep saying, "I am human."

- **Love Yourself** - Love yourself by sticking a sticky note with a positive affirmation on a mirror you see daily. Make sure it's placed so you can read it all the time. Start with a statement like "I am enough" and change it up often to cultivate subliminal love and adoration for yourself. You deserve it.

5
Navigating Relationships With ADHD

W hile attention deficit hyperactivity disorder (ADHD or ADD) symptoms of distractibility, disorganization, and impulsivity can cause issues in many areas of adult life, these symptoms can be especially harmful to your closest relationships. This is particularly true if ADHD symptoms have never received a thorough diagnosis or treatment.

Being the one with ADHD, you could experience frequent criticism, nagging, and micromanagement. Nothing you do appears to satisfy your spouse or lover, regardless of what you try. You shun your partner or say everything necessary to get them off your back since you don't feel appreciated as an adult. You wish your partner would let up just a little and stop trying to manage every area of your life. You are curious about the one you fell in love with.

Being in a relationship with an individual with ADHD can make you feel isolated, underappreciated, and overlooked. You're sick and tired of being the only one in the relationship who must care for things independently. You doubt your ability to rely on your spouse. You are compelled to issue repeated reminders and demands, or else just do the work yourself because they never seem to follow through on their commitments. Sometimes it seems as though the person you're dating just doesn't give a damn.

It is easy to understand how the emotions on both sides could contribute to a negative feedback loop in the relationship. In contrast to the non-ADHD partner's complaints, nagging, and growing resentment, the ADHD partner feels defensive and withdraws after feeling judged and misunderstood. No one is satisfied in the end. However, things don't have to be this way. Understanding how ADHD affects your relationship and how you may make more positive and useful decisions about handling difficulties and interacting with one another will help you create a healthier relationship. These techniques can help you and your partner communicate more effectively and grow closer.

The Impact Of ADHD On Adult Relationships

Understanding how ADHD affects your relationship is the first step towards transforming it. You can discover more effective ways of responding once you can recognize how the symptoms of ADHD are impacting your interactions as a pair. This means the ADHD partner is learning how to control her symptoms. This requires the partner who does not have ADHD to practice responding to their partner's frustrations in ways that uplift and inspire them. Here are some relationship issues that ADHD symptoms can bring on.

Difficulties With Attention

Your partner may feel ignored and undervalued if you lose focus during conversations if you have ADHD. Additionally, you can carelessly agree to something you later regret or omit key information, which can frustrate your loved one.

Forgetfulness

Even when paying attentively, someone with ADHD may later forget what was promised or talked about. Your spouse can begin to believe you don't care or are untrustworthy when it's their birthday or the time to pick up the formula you promised.

A Lack Of Organization

This may result in a lack of productivity and general disorder in the house. Partners may feel as though they are doing an excessive amount of household work and cleaning up after the person with ADHD.

Impulsivity

You might blurt out remarks without thinking if you have ADHD, which might harm people's feelings. This impulsivity can also result in careless and even reckless behavior (such as making a large purchase that wasn't planned for and setting off arguments about money).

Emotional Rants

Many people who have ADHD struggle to control their emotions. You can be easily irritated and find it difficult to hold rational conversations. Your partner could feel they must tread carefully to prevent conflicts from erupting.

Put Yourself In Your Partner's Shoes

Learning to see things from your partner's viewpoint is the first step towards salvaging your relationship. You might believe that you already understand your partner's perspective if you've been together for a while or if you've often had the same arguments. But be mindful of how easy it is to misjudge your partner's behavior and intentions. Even if only one of you has ADHD, you and your partner are more different than you might realize. Furthermore, simply because you have heard it all before does not imply fully understanding what your partner is saying. It can be particularly challenging to maintain objectivity and perspective when emotions are running high, as they often do while dealing with ADHD relationship concerns.

By asking questions and paying attention, you can best imagine yourself in your partner's position. Find a time when you're not already upset to sit down and discuss. Allow your spouse to express their feelings without interjecting to explain or justify yourself. When your partner is finished, summarize what they said and check your understanding by saying it aloud. To help you think about the points later, you might want to write them down. It's your turn after your partner is done. Ask them to do the same for you as you pay attention with open ears and a fresh perspective. Below are some proven ways on how to improve your relationship's understanding.

Learn About ADHD

It will be easier to know how ADHD affects your relationship as you both gain more knowledge about the disorder and its symptoms. You can notice that a light turns on. So many of your problems as a pair are now clear! It can be possible for the non-ADHD partner to take symptoms less personally by remembering that an ADHD brain is hardwired differently from a brain without ADHD. Knowing the cause of some of your behaviors and that there are measures you can take to regulate your symptoms might be a comfort for the partner with ADHD.

Recognize The Effect Your Actions Have On Your Relationship

It's critical to understand how your untreated ADHD symptoms impact your relationship if you are the one who has it. If you're a partner who doesn't have ADHD, think about how your nagging and critiquing make your partner feel. If you don't like how your partner brings it up or responds to you, don't ignore or discount their complaints.

Distinguish Your Partner's Symptoms Or Actions From Who They Are

Consider your partner's forgetfulness and lack of follow-through as signs of ADHD rather than calling them "irresponsible." Remember that symptoms aren't personality traits. The non-ADHD partner also experiences the same thing. Recognize that nagging rarely results from an uncaring partner but rather from feelings of tension and dissatisfaction.

How The Partner With ADHD Often Feels

People with ADHD often perceive the world in a difficult way for others to relate to or understand because their minds are always racing. Here are some ways the partner with ADHD often feels.

- **Overwhelmed By The Ongoing Stress Brought On By ADHD Symptoms, Whether Covertly Or Outwardly** - Much more work is involved in maintaining daily order than most people realize. ADHD can make someone feel like they are fighting to keep their head above water, even though it isn't always obvious.

- **Subservient To Their Partners** - Their partners often rebuke them or take charge of the situation. The criticism makes them feel inept and often fosters a parent-child dynamic. Men may feel emasculated as a result of these interactions.

- **Shamed** - They often conceal a lot of shame, sometimes making up for it with bluster or withdrawal.

- **Unwanted And Unloved** - The constant reminders from partners, employers, and other people that they should "change" just serve to confirm their unlovability as they are.

- **Fearing Further Failure** - There is a greater chance of failure punishment as their relationships deteriorate. But this partner will eventually fall short because of their inconsistent behaviors brought on by ADHD. Reluctance to try is a result of anticipating failure.

- **A Yearning For Acceptance** - People with ADHD often have a strong emotional need to be accepted for their flaws.

How The Non-ADHD Partner Often Feels

- **Unwanted Or Unloved** - Instead of being regarded

as a distraction, the lack of attention is seen as a lack of interest. Being "cherished" and getting the attention from one's spouse that this entails is one of the most popular fantasies.

- **Irate And Emotionally Numb** - Many conversations with the ADHD spouse are tinged with anger and bitterness. This anger can occasionally be seen as disconnected expressions. Some non-ADHD partners try to bury their emotions inside to control hostile confrontations.

- **A Great Deal Of Stress** - The non-ADHD spouse often shoulders the lion's share of the family responsibilities and can never relax. Due to the ADHD spouse's erratic behavior, life could end abruptly at any moment.

- **Offended And Ignored** - A non-ADHD spouse finds it puzzling that the ADHD spouse doesn't act more often on their knowledge and suggestions when it is "clear" what needs to be done.

- **Depleted And Worn Out** - Too many obligations fall on the non-ADHD spouse, and no amount of effort seems to be able to mend the marriage.

- **Frustrated** - A non-ADHD spouse could think that the same problems keep resurfacing (a boomerang effect).

Taking Responsibility For Your Role

It's time to take ownership of your part in the relationship when you've put yourself in your partner's shoes. You can progress once you acknowledge your role in the issues your relationship is experiencing. The non-ADHD partner is also affected by this.

The symptoms of the ADHD partner may be the cause of a problem, but they are not the only factor. How the non-ADHD partner handles the annoying symptom can foster understanding and compromise or lead to misunderstandings and resentment. If you have ADHD, you are responsible for responding to your partner's worries. Your response can make your partner feel heard and affirmed or ignored and rejected.

Break Free From The Child-Parent Dynamic

With the partner without ADHD playing the parent and the partner with ADHD playing the child, many couples feel stuck in an unproductive parent-child connection. It often begins when the partner with ADHD doesn't complete responsibilities, including forgetting to pay the cable bill, piling clean laundry on the bed, or failing to pick up the kids after promising to do so. More and more domestic duties are being assumed by a partner who does not have ADHD.

They grow more resentful as the partnership grows more unbalanced. It becomes more difficult to recognize and value the ADHD spouse's strengths and contributions. The ADHD partner is aware of this, of course. They begin to believe there is no use in making an effort and write off the non-ADHD spouse as demanding and difficult to please. How can you then change this pattern?

Tips For The Non-ADHD Partner

You can't control your spouse but can manage your actions. Stop the nagging and verbal abuse right away. Neither produces outcomes.

As your partner makes strides, congratulate them and recognize their efforts.

Concentrate more on your partner's intentions than their actions when possible. For instance, someone might become distracted while listening to you, but that doesn't imply they don't value what you have to say.

Refrain from trying to "parent" your companion. Both your relationship and your spouse will suffer as a result of it.

Tips For The ADHD Partner

Admit that your ADHD problems are affecting your relationship. It goes beyond the simple fact that your partner is unreasonable. Examine the available therapies. Your companion will be less demanding as you develop the ability to control your symptoms and increase your dependability.

If you and your spouse find that intense emotions are derailing your chats, decide beforehand that you both need to take a break to collect your thoughts and relax.

Look for methods to spoil your partner. Your partner will feel less like your parent if they perceive that you provide for them, even in little ways.

Start Communicating And Stop Fighting

As you've already seen, communication between partners often deteriorates when ADHD is present. One spouse feels overworked. One of them feels under attack. Instead of solving the problem, they wind up arguing with one another.

Do what you can to calm irrational emotions to better communication. If necessary, wait until you are calm before bringing up a topic. Pay attention to what your partner has to say when you're talking. Consider what the fundamental issue in your argument is. What is the bigger problem?

For instance: A couple of fights due to the hour-late dinner. The husband, who does not have ADHD, is upset for reasons other than having nothing to eat. He is annoyed by his wife's unreliability and indifference (I work hard to support her! Why do I never receive any care? She would exert more effort if she cared about me!). The wife with ADHD feels overburdened and unfairly criticized (I have too much housework to do). I'm finding it difficult to stay organized, and I've lost sight of time. How does that make me a bad wife?).

Finding a solution is much easier once you've located the real problem. If the husband in this scenario understood his wife's persistent tardiness and disarray weren't personal, he would be less annoyed. This is a sign of untreated ADHD. The woman will be more motivated to make it happen for her side once she realizes that a punctual meal makes her husband feel cherished and valued.

Don't hold your feelings within. Whatever your feelings may be, be honest about them. Bring things to the surface to resolve them together as a pair.

You can't read people's minds. Don't presume to know what your partner is thinking. Avoid the "if my spouse loved me..."

pitfall. If your partner does something that annoys you, talk to them instead of stewing in silence.

Watch your language and delivery. Avoid using critical language or asking your partner, "How many times do I have to tell you?" or "Why can't you ever do what you said you would?"

Discover the humor in the circumstance. Laugh at the inevitable misconceptions and miscommunications. Laughter eases strain and strengthens your relationship.

How To Communicate Better If You Have ADHD

ADHD symptoms can obstruct communication. You can improve your talks with others and your relationship by using the following advice.

- **When You Can, Talk To People Face To Face** - Nonverbal indicators like eye contact, voice inflection, and gestures convey much more information than words. You must speak to your spouse face-to-face rather than over the phone, text, or email if you want them to understand the emotion hidden beneath the words.

- **Don't Interrupt, And Pay Attention** - Try to keep your eyes on the other person while they are speaking. Repeat their words whenever your attention stops keeping up with the conversation. Try to refrain from interjecting.

- **Ask Questions** - Ask the other person a question instead of launching into whatever is on your mind—or the many things on your mind. They'll know you're paying attention if they see it.

- **Request A Repeat** - As soon as you become aware that your focus has diverted, apologize to the other person and urge them to restate what was just stated. It will become more difficult to reconnect if you let the conversation drag on for too long while your thoughts are elsewhere.

- **Control Your Emotions** - If you find it difficult to talk about some topics without losing your cool or saying something you'll later regret, think about trying mindfulness meditation. Regular mindfulness meditation can give you more control over your emotions and stop the emotional outbursts that can be so harmful to a relationship, in addition to helping to reduce impulsivity and increase attention.

Working Together As A Team

There is no reason why you can't have a healthy, mutually satisfying relationship, even if one spouse has ADHD. The secret is to develop teamwork skills. A healthy relationship entails giving and receiving, with both parties fully cooperating and actively seeking ways to help one another.

- **Spend Some Time Figuring Out What You're Good At And What Challenges You The Most On Both Sides** - If your spouse is strong in a role you aren't, they can step up to the plate, and vice versa. It ought to feel like a fair trade. Think of ways to acquire outside help if you and your partner are weak in the same area. If neither of you is financially savvy, you can hire a bookkeeper or look into money management applications that make budgeting easier.

- **Stick To Your Division Of Labor** - While you manage the kids and the cooking, the partner who doesn't have ADHD may be more suited to take care of the bills and do errands.

- **Plan Weekly Meetings** - Meet once a week to discuss problems and evaluate your development as a couple.

- **Consider The Labor Division** - If one of you is carrying most of the load, list tasks and obligations and rebalance the workload.

- **Outsource, Automate, And Delegate** - You don't have to handle everything by yourself or with your partner. Give your kids chores if you have any. Additionally, you can think about getting a cleaning service, ordering groceries to be delivered, or setting up automatic bill payments.

- **Split Up Specific Tasks If Necessary** - The partner who doesn't have ADHD may need to take over as the "closer" if the partner with ADHD struggles to finish things. To prevent resentments, take this into account in your arrangement.

Make A Workable Plan

You're probably not very good at planning or creating systems if you have ADHD. However, that doesn't imply that you can't stick to a strategy after it has been established. A partner who doesn't have ADHD can greatly help in this area. They can help you create a strategy and routine that will help you stay on top of your obligations.

First, analyze your arguments' most common topics, such as household duties or persistent tardiness. Then consider doable solutions that you can implement. A large wall calendar with checkboxes next to each person's daily activities can be useful for remembering chores. You may create a calendar on your smartphone with timers to remind you of future events if you are often late.

Assisting Your ADHD Partner

- **Establish A Routine** - The additional structure will be advantageous to your companion. Consider setting up specific times for meals, exercise, and sleep, as well as the tasks you and your partner must complete.

- **Put External Reminders In Place** - This can be a to-do list on your phone, a dry-erase board, or sticky notes.

- **Manage The Clutter** - Although people with ADHD often struggle to become and remain orderly, clutter further heightens the sense that their lives are out of control. Assist your partner in creating an organization and clutter-control system.

- **Requests Should Be Repeated To The ADHD Partner** - Ask your partner to reiterate your agreement to prevent misunderstandings.

6
Thriving In The Workplace With ADHD

E mployers look for candidates and employees with excellent focus, attention to detail, quickness, and organization. However, if you have ADHD, doing all of these tasks and more might be quite challenging. It can be hard to put forth good work and keep a job consistently. You might have agitation or difficulty concentrating, typical symptoms of the disorder. However, there are steps you can take to overcome your ADHD and succeed in the workplace. It can occasionally be advantageous.

How Does ADHD Affect Employment?

According to estimates, 8 to 9 million adult Americans have ADHD. And a lot of other people who are in comparable circumstances struggle at work.

In contrast to 72% of individuals without ADHD, just 50% of adults with ADHD could maintain full-time employment, according to a national poll. Even when they managed to land a job, they often made less money than their contemporaries who did not. These employment issues result in annual income losses of close to $77 billion.

The severity of your ADHD will determine how much it affects your employment prospects. Some individuals could just struggle to stay on target, while others struggle to go through the workday without having a major argument with a boss or coworker. Some more badly impacted people may lose jobs, find themselves changing jobs frequently, or need to apply for disability benefits.

ADHD impacts performance at work in a variety of ways. Meetings may be unbearable if you have problems staying focused and can't sit still. It cannot be easy to keep track of numerous projects and deadlines.

According to one study, patients with ADHD often struggled more with verbal fluency, working memory, attention, and other cognitive skills. All of these are executive-function skills, which are crucial in the job.

If you have ADHD, you can find it challenging to manage your time, get and remain organized, pay attention, follow instructions, finish tasks, pay attention to details, arrive at work on time, speak only when it's your turn to speak, sit quietly, and maintain emotional control.

Additionally, you can struggle with procrastination and wrath.

Depression and low self-esteem are common side effects of ADHD. These feelings may worsen if you cannot meet deadlines and finish your assignment on time.

How Can You Get And Keep A Job?

Many fidgety adults who have trouble focusing or have other symptoms have never received an official diagnosis of ADHD. Consultation with a medical professional specializing in adult ADHD should be your first step if you have any of the abovementioned issues. They can speak with you to find out whether you do have it. And if you do, get diagnosed so you can begin the appropriate course of treatment.

Medication, therapy, or a combination of the two can help people. You can practice organizational techniques after learning them from a coach or occupational therapist.

Work with a career counselor to identify the position that most closely matches your interests, needs, and skills if you are about to begin your job hunt. That could look for faster-paced work, more flexible hours, and a looser structure. Alternatively, you might wish to launch your own company so that you can choose your working conditions and hours.

Try these things when you land a job:

- **Make Peace** - Ask to work in a quiet place where you won't be easily distracted.

- **Team Up** - Work with a structured manager or coworker who can help you see initiatives through to completion.

- **Plan It** - Keep a day planner that includes a calendar and a to-do list. Continue to update them. Make plans to get electronic reminders for appointments and due dates from your computer or smartphone.

- **Put It In Writing** - During meetings and phone calls, make notes and list any new duties.

- **Schedule Interruption** - Plan specific times to respond to voicemail and email daily to prevent distraction.

- **Set Attainable Goals** - Organize your days into discrete tasks, and only attempt to do one at a time. Set a timer to help you know when to move on to the next task.

- **Gratify Yourself** - Find a way to treat yourself after you finish a task, or use these time-management tips. Go for a stroll during a break. Read an article from a magazine. For major goals, treat yourself to a special lunch or purchase something you've been craving.

- **Delegate** - Get an assistant or intern to handle the little things if you can to free up your time so you can concentrate on the larger picture.

- **Make It A Habit To Relax** - Develop your relaxing skills. They can help in improving concentration. Try deep breathing or meditation. Every hour, get up to go for a stroll, get a drink of water, or chat with a coworker.

Hire a career counselor or executive coach to help you adjust to your new position. They can provide you with advice on any problems you run into. They can also assist you in resolving the problematic work scenarios you encounter. For instance, they could assist you in role-playing how to talk about a salary raise with your supervisor without the discussion becoming tense.

Super Strengths Of ADHD Adults You Need To Know

Few individuals think adults with ADHD have strengths because of how society views the disorder. You may also be disheartened because you only perceive weaknesses with ADHD. But you also need to be aware of ADHD's advantages. Many entrepreneurs and celebrities with ADHD succeed thanks to these traits of ADHD adults.

ADHD is often viewed as a drawback. People notice this because they only pay attention to flaws. You should be aware of the shortcomings of adults with ADHD. Just be careful not to let your flaws consume you. Don't only focus on your flaws. To succeed in any environment, identify and learn the strengths of adults with ADHD.

Creativity

A mind that is constantly thinking and creating is a mind that is never at rest. Creative energies are necessary for growth. Unsurprisingly, adults with ADHD thrive on and produce creative energy.

Some individuals believe that people with ADHD greatly benefit from their artistic skills. This is how you ought to view creativity as well. Adults with ADHD often think outside the box. They flourish in situations that call for creative thought. The creative energies of many people with ADHD benefit countless enterprises and our society.

Innovation

Adults with ADHD like to push the envelope. Adults with ADHD often become bored and quickly distracted. While in certain cases, distraction and boredom ruin careers. In other cases, they spark remarkable inventions and scientific achievements.

One of the enormous advantages that people with ADHD have is innovation. Adults with ADHD have trouble accepting the way things are. To reiterate, this can destroy a career track professional in the wrong industry.

Adults with ADHD should avoid employment that involves intricate duties, a lot of organization, or that keeps them confined to a desk all day. Some of the worst careers for restless minds include being an accountant or an administrative assistant.

On the other hand, people with ADHD who are innovative and creative can excel in creative industries. Adults with ADHD may consider occupations that require ingenuity, such as acting, self-employment, and sales. The best careers for adults with ADHD are those in this category.

Hyperfocus

Many people with ADHD struggle greatly when they are unable to focus. However, the opposite of lack of focus is hyperfocus, which appears to be one of the strengths of individuals with ADHD. Adults with ADHD may find it difficult to pay attention to particular activities. Other hobbies snag adults with ADHD and won't let go.

You must develop the skill to employ hyperfocus to its full potential. To use hyperfocus to your advantage, you must figure out how to manage and harness your ADHD.

Many problem-solving-oriented jobs lend themselves well to hyperfocus. Science and technology-related careers benefit greatly from the participant's capacity for hyperfocus. Adults with ADHD do well in their careers as scientists, game and computer developers, or athletes. Entrepreneur David Neeleman and professional golfer Bubba Watson are two examples of hyperfocused people with ADHD.

Exuberance

The high energy that takes up most of their day is lamented by many parents of children with ADHD. Just keeping up with their hyperactive toddler is a problem for them. However, when used effectively, high energy can be one of people with ADHD's major assets.

High energy, combined with hyperfocus, gives some researchers and inventors the drive to keep working long after their peers give up. Unfocused hyperactivity can overburden the dynamics of a household. However, high energy drives successful jobs and creative forces when properly channeled.

Efficiency

One of the main outcomes of hyperfocus and high energy is another one of ADHD people's productivity strengths. While adults with ADHD struggle with boredom and low productivity, the opposite can occur under the right circumstances: high productivity levels.

Adults with ADHD can accomplish outcomes at a special rate when focusing on a crucial problem. Adults with ADHD have an active mind, constantly switching between tasks and thoughts.

For most ADHD people, focusing and directing their mental energy is key to enhancing productivity. With the right management, productivity can become a major asset, and you could even claim that ADHD boosted your productivity.

The Positive Side Of ADHD At Work

If you work for a larger organization, they are prohibited from discriminating against you because of your condition because ADHD is regarded as a disability under the Americans with Disabilities Act. The law also mandates that your employer meet your needs. However, you must feel comfortable disclosing to your employer that you have ADHD. Doing more research on this subject could be helpful before bringing it up so you have a strategy.

Finally, benefit from ADHD's potential advantages—yes, there are advantages. The relentless drive to try new things, restlessness, and impulsivity can be wonderful traits. This is particularly valid if you operate your own company.

According to studies, many adults with ADHD become business owners. Finding a career that fits you best is the key to success. Then, to maximize your job, employ your drive, inventiveness, and other strengths.

Conclusion

A DHD can negatively impact performance at work or school and personal relationships if it is not properly diagnosed and managed.

It's challenging to have ADHD as an adult. But with the right lifestyle changes and care, you can significantly lessen your symptoms and enhance your quality of life.

Adult ADHD coping mechanisms can help individuals overcome the issues that impulsivity, hyperactivity, and inattention can lead to. Eliminating distractions while driving can improve safety while adding reminders to your calendar can help you remember things, and organizing your environment can help you avoid losing important items.

A person's symptoms, medical history, and, occasionally, the findings of psychological testing are used by doctors to make an ADHD diagnosis. People who obtain a diagnosis can benefit from medications and other forms of treatment to control the condition.

When you have ADHD, you can modify your schedule and finish things in various ways. The good news is that they extend beyond what you've read in this book. If you find it difficult to stay on track, a mental health expert can help you develop solutions for your needs.